FRIENDS OF THE
HILLCREST LIBRARY

© Maurice Sendak 1995

This book
has been donated
by

Karen and Darren Ruth

in honor of

J.J. and Trevor Ruth
2004

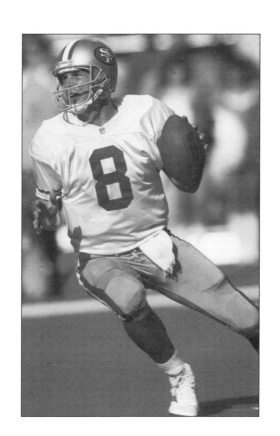

CREATIVE EDUCATION

SAN FRANCISCO 49ERS

JULIE NELSON

Published by Creative Education
123 South Broad Street, Mankato, Minnesota 56001
Creative Education is an imprint of The Creative Company

Designed by Rita Marshall

Photos by: Allsport USA, Bettmann/CORBIS, SportsChrome

Library of Congress Cataloging-in-Publication Data

Nelson, Julie.
San Francisco 49ers / by Julie Nelson.
p. cm. — (NFL today)
Summary: Traces the history of the team from its beginnings through 1999.
ISBN 1-58341-059-7

1. San Francisco 49ers (Football team)—History—Juvenile literature.
[1. San Francisco 49ers (Football team)—History. 2. Football—History.] I. Title.
II. Title: San Francisco Forty-niners. III. Series: NFL today (Mankato, Minn.)

GV956.S3N45   2000
796.332'64'0979461—dc21   99-015756

9 8 7 6 5 4 3 2

To many Americans, San Francisco, California, is a city of mystery and romance. A popular spot for vacationers and honeymoon couples, this coastal city offers unique sights and sounds ranging from breathtaking views of the Pacific Ocean to the clang of trolley car bells. Fishermen's Wharf, the Barbary Coast, and the Golden Gate Bridge are just a few of the well-known landmarks in San Francisco, one of America's most beautiful cities. The San Francisco 49ers are also a landmark of sorts, for San Francisco was the first city west of the Rocky Mountains to be given a professional football franchise.

One of the first 49ers stars, Hugh McElhenny.

Skilled and speedy return man Len Eshmont averaged more than 26 yards per kickoff return.

The history of the 49ers began in 1946, when the new All-America Football Conference established a franchise in San Francisco. Two brothers, Tony and Vic Morabito, had worked hard to establish a football team in the Bay area. Led primarily by Tony, the team prospered in its first four seasons in the AAFC, going a combined 39–15–2.

Although the 49ers were doing well, the All-America Football Conference was not, and the league folded in 1949. Luckily for Tony Morabito, the National Football League offered to let four AAFC franchises join the NFL. One of those teams was the San Francisco 49ers, named for the gold seekers who settled around San Francisco in 1849 during the California gold rush. Morabito hired a new coaching staff and then began looking for players to open the 1950 NFL season. He intended to make the 49ers a winning team for his beloved San Francisco.

A SUCCESSFUL BEGINNING

The 49ers' first coach in the NFL, Lawrence "Buck" Shaw, was put in charge of recruiting the talent that would fill the team's roster. Many of those players were men that the established NFL teams had cut because they were considered too old or not talented enough. Buck Shaw set out to surprise the league by molding this collection of players into a winning squad.

One of Shaw's first choices in building the new 49ers was a small, left-handed quarterback named Frankie Albert, who joined the team in 1950. After playing with the 49ers for several seasons, he would later return to coach the team from

Defensive tackle Bryant Young dominated with his strength.

Quarterback Y.A. Tittle emerged as a star, passing for 20 touchdowns.

1956 to 1958. Albert's backup in his first year in San Francisco was Yelberton Abraham Tittle, better known as Y.A. Tittle.

Tittle, who emerged as a standout quarterback with the 49ers and later with the New York Giants, became famous for his "alley-oop" passes to athletic halfback R.C. Owens under the goal posts. As one newspaperman said, "It's the strangest thing I've ever seen on a football field." Owens, a former basketball star, would gauge Tittle's throw, jump as high as he needed to snag the pass, and come down in the end zone for a touchdown.

Shaw also signed running back Hugh McElhenny, who joined the team in 1952. In just his first game in a 49ers uniform, McElhenny earned a nickname: "the King." During that game, Frankie Albert came to the sidelines and told Coach Shaw that McElhenny refused to carry the ball unless he could have a play created just for him. "He's the king," Albert told Shaw. "McElhenny is the king of runners." The nickname stuck.

But McElhenny wasn't the only star in the San Francisco backfield with a catchy nickname. Shaw also snagged Joe "the Jet" Perry, who ran for more than 1,000 yards in 1953 and 1954 and scored an astounding 50 rushing touchdowns. With such players as the confident McElhenny and speedy Perry, San Francisco put together six straight winning seasons between 1951 and 1956.

The 1957 season was again a winning one. Unfortunately, it ended on a sad note. At halftime of a Chicago Bears-49ers game, the last contest of the season, team president Tony Morabito, who had been watching the game, died of a heart attack. The players, stunned by the news, went back out on the field and won the game 27–17 in memory of the owner. Unfortunately, the 49ers then blew a 27–7 lead over Detroit to lose 31–27 in the playoffs.

A Change of Fortune

Defensive tackle Leo Nomellini earned his sixth straight Pro Bowl berth.

The San Francisco 49ers had managed to scratch out some success in their earlier years, but the period between 1959 and 1967 was a frustrating one. Although they consistently ended up at or above the .500 mark, the 49ers rarely finished higher than third or fourth place in the NFL's tough Western Division.

One 49ers star who shined during this time was John Brodie, the team's quarterback. Brodie came to San Francisco in 1957 from Stanford University via the NFL draft. By the time he finally left the club in 1973, he had led the league in various years in passing completions, yardage, and touchdowns and had won the 1970 Most Valuable Player award. Through those years, Brodie remained in San Francisco even though other teams frequently tempted him with offers of higher salaries.

San Francisco also had a defensive line that knew what it meant to wreak havoc with an opponent's game plan. Defensive tackle Charlie Krueger joined the 49ers in 1959 and anchored the front line for the next 15 years.

But determination and raw talent aside, the San Francisco 49ers did not have the ingredients they needed for real success in the NFL. Although they had winning seasons and treated their fans to some outstanding games, something was still missing.

9

A longtime 49ers star, tight end Brent Jones.

Clutch receiver John Taylor.

1 9 6 9

Rookie receiver Gene Washington led San Francisco in catches (51).

In 1967, a new head coach arrived in San Francisco. Dick Nolan, a quiet, wiry Irishman, had an impressive playing and coaching resume when he came to the 49ers. After playing defensive back for the New York Giants and St. Louis Cardinals, he had helped coach Tom Landry build the Dallas Cowboys into winners.

Under Nolan, the 49ers gradually climbed from the bottom to the top of the divisional standings. Offensively, much of the credit went to John Brodie, who sparked a San Francisco offense that was one of the highest-scoring in the league. Also powering the 49ers were dynamic wide receiver Gene Washington, dependable tight end Ted Kwalick, and durable running back Ken Willard.

Coach Nolan's passion, however, was defense, and he worked feverishly to develop young but talented players. Among these skilled defenders were end Cedrick Hardman, linebacker Dave Wilcox, and cornerback Bruce Taylor. For experience and on-field leadership, Nolan relied on veteran defensive back Jimmy Johnson.

Drafted from UCLA in the first round of the 1961 NFL draft, Johnson remained in San Francisco until 1976. In a career that spanned 16 seasons, Johnson made 47 career interceptions and returned them for nearly 615 yards. An athlete who was capable of playing any number of positions, Johnson played wide receiver in 1962 and cornerback in 1963 and was named All-Pro four times.

Despite all of their talent, the San Francisco 49ers were still unable to win consistently during Dick Nolan's tenure. Victory always seemed within the 49ers' reach, only to be snatched out of their hands.

A good example of this was the thriller played on December 23, 1972, between the 49ers and Tom Landry's Dallas Cowboys in the NFC playoffs. As the fourth quarter began, Dallas trailed 28–13. The Cowboys then reeled off 17 points to win 30–28 and destroy the 49ers' dreams of a Super Bowl.

STARTING OVER

In 1977, the Morabito family announced that they wanted to sell the 49ers. Edward DeBartolo Jr., the son of an Ohio family that had made money building shopping malls, soon raised the $17-million asking price for the club and bought it. DeBartolo then announced to the press that he intended to do whatever was needed to make his team a winner.

1 9 7 2

Cornerback Jimmy Johnson intercepted four passes to lead the defense.

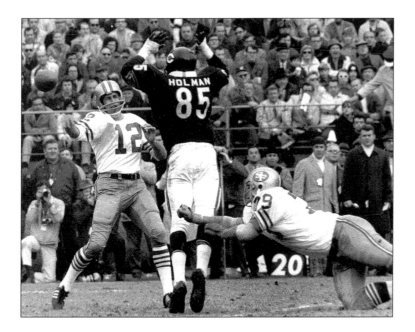

Fearless quarterback John Brodie.

But nothing could turn the 49ers around in 1978 and '79. Two consecutive 2–14 seasons and four coaches in three years convinced DeBartolo that he needed to make drastic changes in his game plan.

The fifth coach DeBartolo hired was just what the hurting team needed. Bill Walsh, a college professor who had never played pro football, took the reins of the team in 1979. Walsh did have coaching experience with several pro teams before coaching at Stanford in 1977 and 1978 and winning two bowl games in a row. When DeBartolo called and offered him the head coaching position in San Francisco, Walsh eagerly accepted. As the next 10 years proved, DeBartolo was a very good judge of football talent.

It was a slow start, however. When Walsh first arrived, the 49ers had spent two years in the NFC cellar, and even the usually optimistic Walsh had his doubts. "I'll be honest with you," he told reporters. "Turning this team around will be no easy matter. It's going to take time."

1 9 8 0

Under Bill Walsh's guidance, San Francisco climbed to a 6–10 record.

THE BEST IN THE BUSINESS

That turnaround would happen much quicker than anyone could have predicted. Within three short years, Walsh's 49ers rose from the bottom of the standings to the top of the football world.

This dramatic improvement was made possible by Walsh's sharp eye for talent, which brought many new faces to San Francisco. Receiver Dwight Clark, safety Ronnie Lott, linebacker Keena Turner, cornerback Eric Wright, and others arrived via the NFL draft. Linebacker Jack Reynolds and

Safety Ronnie Lott was a punishing hitter.

Unstoppable pass rusher Cedrick Hardman (#86).

defensive end Fred Dean were also acquired through key trades. Much of the credit, however, was due to a young quarterback from Notre Dame.

Joe Montana was born in Monogahela, Pennsylvania, an area that had produced other great quarterbacks including George Blanda, Johnny Unitas, and Joe Namath. As a child, Montana showed a special aptitude for sports, excelling in both football and baseball.

At his parents' urging, Montana decided to attend The University of Notre Dame, home of the Fighting Irish. When he showed up for freshman practice, he found that he was no longer the star, but rather the seventh-string quarterback. Montana saw little playing time during his first year. As a sophomore, however, he broke out in a crucial game against North Carolina, throwing for 129 yards and 15 points in the game's final minute.

Montana went on to record many more astonishing saves at Notre Dame. In the 1979 Cotton Bowl against the University of Houston—Montana's final college game—Houston led the Fighting Irish 34–13 in the third quarter. In a miraculous comeback, Montana ran, passed, and fought his way to a 35–34 Notre Dame victory.

Still, many NFL coaches thought that Montana was too small for the pros. Not selected until the third round of the NFL draft by San Francisco, the young quarterback set out to prove his critics wrong. It didn't take long.

During his 14 years with the 49ers, Montana established himself as more than a premier quarterback. He became "Joe Cool," a living legend renowned for his ability to perform at his best in the most critical moments of big games. Montana

1 9 8 1

Sure-handed end Dwight Clark set a new team record with 85 catches.

Roger Craig shared Montana's never-say-die attitude (pages 18-19).   17

1 9 8 8

Roger Craig had a career season, setting a new 49ers record with 1,502 rushing yards.

led San Francisco to four Super Bowl victories—in 1982 over Cincinnati (26–21), in 1985 over Miami (38–16), in 1988 over Cincinnati again (20–16), and in 1989 over Denver (55–10). The final two triumphs put the 49ers alongside the Pittsburgh Steelers and Green Bay Packers as the only teams in NFL history to win back-to-back Super Bowls.

Along the way, Montana made some personal NFL history of his own. He became the only player ever to be named the Most Valuable Player in the Super Bowl three times. He also won the regular-season Most Valuable Player award in 1989 and 1990. By the end of his career, Montana ranked among the top five NFL quarterbacks of all time in passing yards, completions, and touchdown passes. "He's the kingpin, the reason we've been able to maintain this," explained 49ers safety Ronnie Lott.

Montana led the 49ers, but he didn't win four Super Bowls alone. Running backs Roger Craig and Tom Rathman, receivers Jerry Rice and John Taylor, and cornerback Don Griffin were just a few of the other talented players who made the 49ers the most dominant team of the 1980s. "Sure we have some great individual players," commented All-Pro wide receiver Jerry Rice, "but so do many other teams. What we have that is unique is a collective desire to be the best football team ever."

Rice himself was a perfect example of the blending of individual greatness with the 49ers' team concept. A number one draft pick out of Mississippi Valley State in 1985, Rice quickly established himself as a major star by winning the league's Most Valuable Player Award in 1987. He went on to break every major NFL career receiving record and to become the consensus choice as the greatest wide receiver in NFL history. Still, this star of stars never clamored for attention. Like his teammates, he just earned it on the field.

YOUNG TAKES THE TORCH

R ice and his fellow 49ers faced a new challenge in 1991. The aging Montana had suffered an elbow injury and was out for the entire season; he would ultimately be traded to the Kansas City Chiefs. Clearly, it was time for a new quarterback to take the reins in San Francisco.

Perennial All-Pro safety Ronnie Lott led the 49ers with five interceptions.

Steve Young had served as a backup to Montana for four years. But San Francisco fans—accustomed to the brilliance of Montana—were skeptical about their new quarterback.

Steve Young was twice named league MVP.

21

Quarterback legend Joe Montana.

Young wasted little time in winning fans over. In 1991, he led the NFL in passing efficiency with 2,517 yards and 17 touchdowns. The 49ers failed to make the playoffs, but Young was on his way. The next year, he was named the NFL's Most Valuable Player and started for the NFC in the Pro Bowl. Young was named league MVP again in 1994 and led the NFL in passing efficiency for the fourth straight year, breaking the old record set by Montana.

Defensive end Charles Haley led the club in sacks (16) for the fifth season in a row.

After all of these feats, however, one key accomplishment was still missing from Young's resume: a Super Bowl victory. The 49ers soon took a big stride toward filling that void by signing free agent cornerback Deion Sanders. Nicknamed "Prime Time," the flashy Sanders grabbed six interceptions—three of which he returned for touchdowns—during the 1994 season. For his heroics, Sanders was named the NFL Defensive Player of the Year.

With Young leading the offense and Sanders sparking the defense, San Francisco was ready for a memorable postseason. After having lost to Dallas in two straight NFC championship games, the 49ers beat the Cowboys 38–28 in the 1994 title game. Two weeks later, the 49ers trounced the San Diego Chargers 49–26 in Super Bowl XXIX. Young set a Super Bowl record with six touchdown passes—surpassing the old mark of five by Montana—and was named the game's Most Valuable Player. After the game, a jubilant Young, who had often been unfavorably compared to Montana because of his failure to win an NFL title, told the media with relief, "I've got the monkey off my back at last." The win was the 49ers' NFL-best fifth Super Bowl victory.

1 9 9 5

Jerry Rice caught 122 passes for 1,848 yards—an NFL record.

An injury to Young and the departure of Sanders to rival Dallas slowed down the 49ers in 1995. By the standards of most franchises, they enjoyed an exceptional year, winning the NFC Western Division with an 11–5 record. A first-round playoff loss to the Green Bay Packers, however, ended the season on a sour note.

That sour note seemed to echo for several seasons, as Green Bay would top San Francisco in the postseason year after year. The 49ers finished 1996 with a 12–4 record even though Young struggled with injuries for much of the season. After dispatching Philadelphia 14–0 in the first round of the playoffs, the 49ers were crushed 35–14 by Green Bay.

Speedy free safety Merton Hanks.

The 49ers' injury problems continued the following season, as Jerry Rice suffered a knee injury in the 1997 season opener at Tampa Bay. It was the first major injury in Rice's illustrious career. "I used to take football for granted," Rice explained. "Every time I'd put the uniform on, I felt like Superman. I'm not invincible anymore."

Steve Young also started the season with a concussion—his third head injury in two years. He dispelled any doubts about his health, though, by passing for 3,029 yards and 19 touchdowns on the season. With Rice injured, big receivers J.J. Stokes and Terrell Owens combined for 1,669 yards, while Garrison Hearst ran for 1,019 yards to power San Francisco's ground game. Another young star who made a name for himself in 1997 was defensive tackle Dana Stubblefield, who finished the year with 15 sacks and Defensive Player of the Year honors.

San Francisco was led from the sidelines in 1997 by rookie coach Steve Mariucci. Formerly the head coach at the University of California, Mariucci was hired after the retirement of coach George Seifert, who finished with a .755 winning percentage and 108 wins in eight seasons in San Francisco. Mariucci quickly proved himself a worthy successor by guiding the 49ers to a 13–3 regular-season record, including an 11-game winning streak—the most ever under a rookie coach.

Although doctors had told the 49ers that Rice would need as much as six months of rehabilitation after his injury, the receiver was back on the field in about half that time. Rice caught a 14-yard pass against Denver to become the first non-kicker in NFL history to score 1,000 career points; unfortunately, he also reinjured his knee, ending his season.

1 9 9 7

Receiver J.J. Stokes bounced back from injuries to rack up 733 total yards.

Big-play receiver Terrell Owens (pages 26-27).

49ers coach Steve Mariucci led his team to a winning record for the 16th straight season.

Despite again losing their veteran superstar, the 49ers made a valiant postseason effort. "It was like the [Chicago] Bulls not having Michael Jordan," explained Mariucci. "They could still win without him, but you'd have a better chance with him." Once again, San Francisco faced off against the Green Bay Packers in the NFC championship game. Once again, amid windy and rainy conditions, the 49ers fell, this time by a 23–10 score.

After the season, San Francisco lost defensive standouts Stubblefield and Kevin Greene to free agency, but Rice returned after two surgeries. Along with Stokes and Owens, Rice helped to form one of the NFL's most dangerous receiving trios. Over the course of the season, the three combined for 3,024 yards and 31 touchdowns. San Francisco's powerful offense also featured Hearst, who broke out for a career-high 1,570 rushing yards in 1998.

Boasting one of the most productive offenses in the league, the 49ers finished the 1998 season 12–4 and again headed into the playoffs to meet their nemesis, Green Bay.

After an exhausting battle between the two teams, the outcome looked bleak for the 49ers, who trailed by four points with only three seconds on the clock. Echoing the heroics of Joe Montana, however, Steve Young then rifled a 25-yard pass to Terrell Owens, who had struggled throughout the game with four dropped passes and a fumble. Young's final pass hit the mark, and Owens held on to win the game.

Unfortunately, the 49ers' Super Bowl run ended the following week at the hands of the upstart Atlanta Falcons. Although the game again went down to the wire, Atlanta took

Versatile running back Charlie Garner.

The greatest receiver in NFL history, Jerry Rice.

A fearsome tackler, All-Pro linebacker Ken Norton Jr.   31

Hard-hitting safety Lance Schulters reminded 49ers fans of former great Ronnie Lott.

advantage of three second-half interceptions to pull out the 20–18 victory.

In 1999, San Francisco fell hard in the standings. There were several reasons for the decline. Many of the team's stars were aging; star halfback Garrison Hearst missed the year after ankle surgery; and Young suffered a concussion that ended his season and put his NFL future in doubt. Although newly acquired running back Charlie Garner stepped in to rush for more than 1,000 yards, the once-mighty 49ers finished the season a dismal 4–12. "We are going to fix this as soon as possible," Mariucci assured fans after the season. "We have a lot of areas to improve."

With the future of longtime stars such as Young and Rice in question, the 49ers are a team with an uncertain future. Although the proud franchise has fallen from its championship ways, the rebuilding effort has begun with the addition of such young players as linebacker Julian Peterson and cornerback Ahmed Plummer. San Francisco fans know that if any team knows how to build a winner, it is their 49ers.